NATIONAL GEOGRAPHIC

BLAZING New Trails

PIONEER EDITION

By Dana Jensen and Peter Winkler

CONTENTS

Face of History. *This actor plays Sacagawea in the movie* Lewis & Clark: Great Journey West.

WHO WAS SACAGAWEA?

By Dana Jensen

THE WIND WHIPPED through the girl's hair. The horse was galloping fast, and she held on tight. Where was she going and what would happen to her? She did not know.

A New Life

The girl was a Native American named Sacagawea. It was around the year 1800. She was about 12 years old. People from another group were taking her away. She lived with them for a few years before she married a fur trader.

Her life changed again in 1804 when she met two **explorers**, Meriwether Lewis and William Clark. Their job was to make maps of the new land in the West.

The men knew Sacagawea could help them because she could speak to other Native Americans. She could be an **interpreter**. In 1805, they asked her and her husband to come along. Sacagawea was just 17 years old.

Into the Wild

Their trip began in April 1805. Sacagawea, the only woman on the team, brought her baby son with her.

A month later, a storm hit. One of the boats started to sink, and tools and papers fell out. Sacagawea grabbed them from the water, saving valuable equipment and knowledge.

Young Explorer. *Sacagawea's son went with her on the trip.*

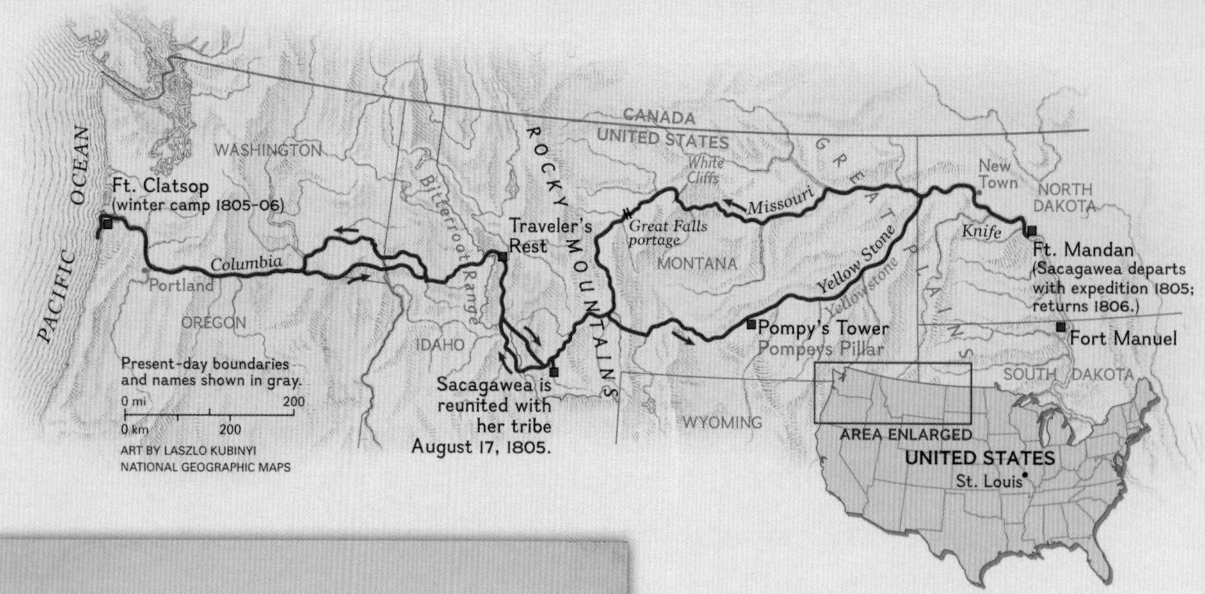

TRAIL OF DISCOVERY

April 1803: France sells the Louisiana Territory to the United States.

July 1803: President Thomas Jefferson hires Lewis and Clark to explore the new land.

May 1804: Lewis and Clark leave St. Louis to begin the trip west.

April 1805: Lewis and Clark ask Sacagawea to join their team.

August 1805: Sacagawea and her brother meet again.

November 1805: The group reaches the Pacific Northwest.

March 1806: The group starts the trip back home.

August 1806: Sacagawea returns to her home village.

September 1806: Lewis and Clark end their trip in St. Louis.

A Very Long Trip

The team reached Sacagawea's old home in August. Sacagawea's brother, who was the chief, was happy to see her. She traded with him for horses to help the team cross the mountains.

The team kept riding west to the ocean. There they built a fort for the winter, in an area that is now Oregon.

It was wet and cold, and food ran low. Luckily, they heard about a dead whale. It could give them meat to eat. Sacagawea and the men found it on the beach.

Actors play Lewis and Clark.

Hard Hike. *Sacagawea never complained. Her strength amazed the men of the team.*

Home, Sweet Home

In March 1806, the team headed home. Sacagawea knew a shorter way through the mountains and showed the group this route.

In August, she arrived home. The team had traveled for sixteen months and covered thousands of miles. Lewis and Clark said farewell; then they traveled on to St. Louis.

Sacagawea had a baby daughter soon after getting home, but then this brave young woman died. No one knows how. Clark was fond of Sacagawea's son. So he took care of her children after her death. He called the boy Pomp, which means "leader" in the language of Sacagawea's people.

Sacagawea's Legacy

Sacagawea contributed a lot to the team. She made peace with many people, traded with them, and found food.

We have many statues of her today because she is an important part of **history**. This young woman was courageous, strong, and helpful. She was a leading lady.

WORDWISE

explorer: person who visits a place to learn about it

history: the study of the past

interpreter: person who tells what is being said in another language

Tale *from the* TRAIL

A Play by Peter Winkler

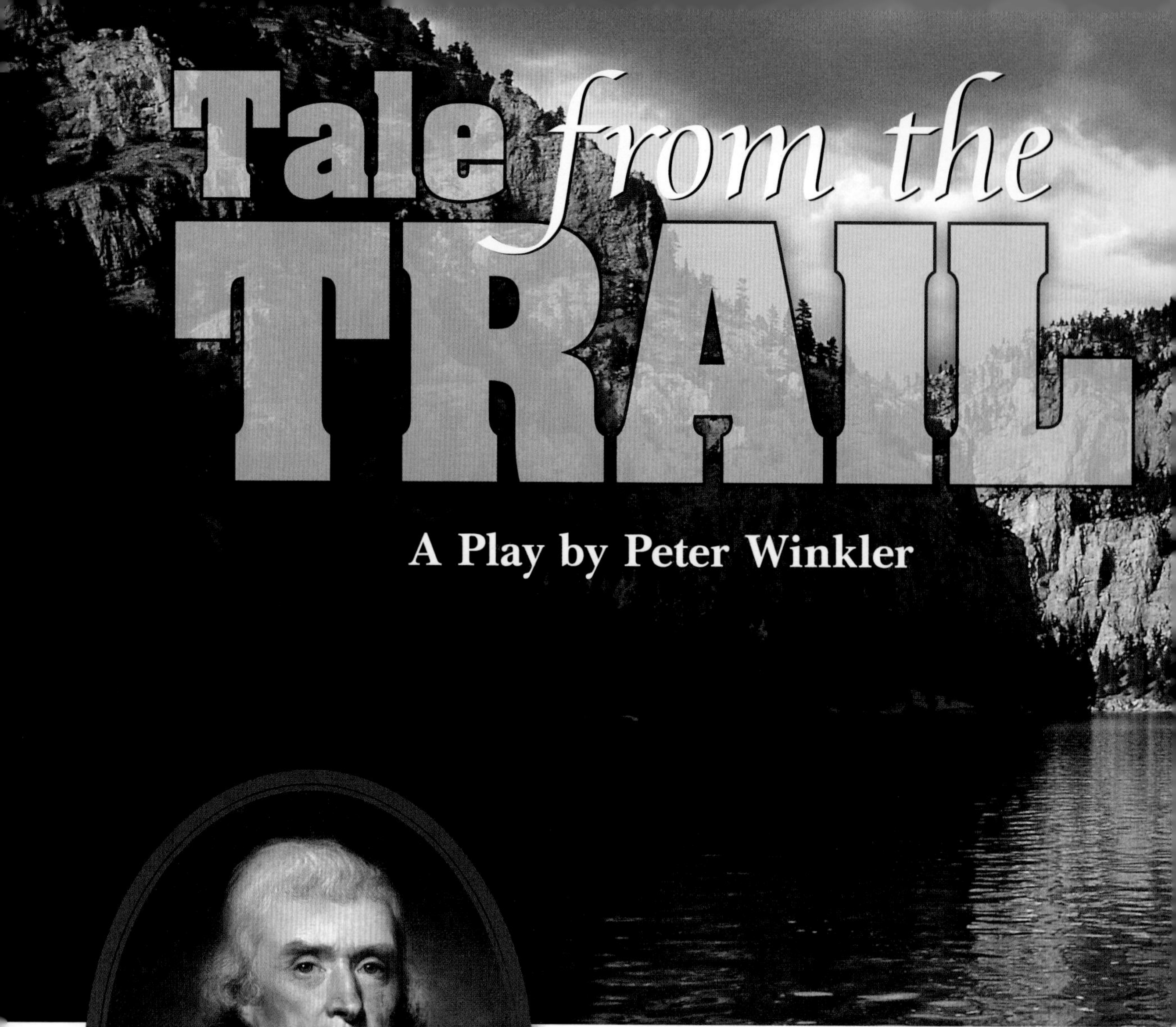

President Thomas Jefferson

The Lewis and Clark team is in for a big surprise. Relive it in this play.

President Thomas Jefferson asked Meriwether Lewis to explore the lands west of the Mississippi River. Lewis asked his friend, William Clark, to help him. They led a team to the Pacific Ocean.

Sacagawea (sak uh juh WEE uh) joined them along the way. She was a woman of the Shoshone (shuh SHOW nee) people from Idaho.

The play is set in August 1805. Lewis and Clark are in the Bitterroot Mountains of Montana and Idaho.

"Gates of the Rocky Mountains." *That's what Meriwether Lewis called the Montana landscape. His team paddled their canoes on this part of the Missouri River in July 1805.*

CHARACTERS

Cameahwait, *Shoshone chief*

Toussaint Charbonneau, *interpreter*

William Clark, *captain*

George Drouillard, *interpreter*

Jumping Fish, *Shoshone teen*

Meriwether Lewis, *captain*

Hugh McNeal, *soldier*

John Ordway, *sergeant*

Sacagawea, *Shoshone interpreter*

John Shields, *soldier*

Shoshone Woman

Shoshone Girl

Scene 1: Big Job

(Lewis, Drouillard (dru YAR), Shields, and McNeal enter and stand on one side of the stage.)

Lewis: We have a big job, men. We must find some Indians! Captain Clark is leading the rest of our team up the river. We'll meet them soon.

McNeal: We've met lots of Indians. Why is it so important to meet more?

Lewis: Horses.

McNeal: I don't understand, captain.

Shields: Look at these mountains! We need horses to carry our gear, and there's only one way to get horses.

Wild Ride. *It was a challenge to get through the Rocky Mountains. The team couldn't carry all its gear on foot. They needed to meet Indians and trade for horses.*

Drouillard: And that way is to trade with the Indians.

(The explorers walk and look around.)

McNeal: Sacagawea says that her people live nearby, doesn't she?

Lewis: Yes. They're called the Shoshone Indians, but she hasn't seen them in several years. Not since a raiding party kidnapped her.

Drouillard: Poor thing. She must have been scared. Then she married that French trader, Charbonneau (shahr buh NOH).

Shields: He's no good. I can't believe he's part of our team.

Lewis: Watch your tongue!

Shields: I'm sorry, captain. At least he brought Sacagawea. She's strong and she's tough.

McNeal: I've never seen her show fear.

Drouillard: I've never seen her show any feelings.

Lewis: That's enough talk. We don't want to scare any Indians. Maybe the Shoshone have never met white people, and they might think we're enemies.

(The explorers walk silently and look around. A Shoshone woman and girl enter and watch carefully from a distance.)

Scene 2: First Contact

(The Shoshone whisper to each other.)

Shoshone Girl: Those are not our people.

Shoshone Woman: No. I don't recognize them.

Shoshone Girl: Have they come to attack us?

Shoshone Woman: I don't know. Sit down and maybe they won't see us.

(The Shoshone sit with arms crossed and heads bowed. Lewis soon sees them. He and his men stop and whisper.)

Lewis: Do you see them?

Others: Yes.

Lewis: Wait here. I'm going to them—slowly. McNeal, hand me the flag. Shields, find me some beads.

(Shields hangs beads around Lewis's neck, and McNeal gives him a U.S. flag. Lewis holds it up as he walks forward.)

Lewis: I am not an enemy. I have come to trade with you.

(Lewis reaches the Indians and gently touches the woman's arm, asking her to stand. The girl watches, and then she stands, too. Lewis gives them each a string of beads.)

Lewis: My name is Meriwether Lewis. I am a friend, not an enemy.

Shoshone Girl: You are?

Lewis: Yes. My people live in the east. Our leader, Thomas Jefferson, sent me to explore this land.

Shoshone Girl: What do you want with us?

Lewis: I want to meet your chief.

Shoshone Woman: Well, you didn't hurt or kill us, so I trust you. Come and meet our people.

(Lewis waves his men over and everyone exits together.)

Scene 3: Where Are They?

(Clark, Charbonneau, Ordway, Sacagawea, and any extra explorers enter. They mime paddling canoes as they move across stage. Sacagawea is stone-faced.)

Charbonneau: I'm so tired. Can't we stop for a while?

Ordway: You lazy lump of stone! You do nothing but complain.

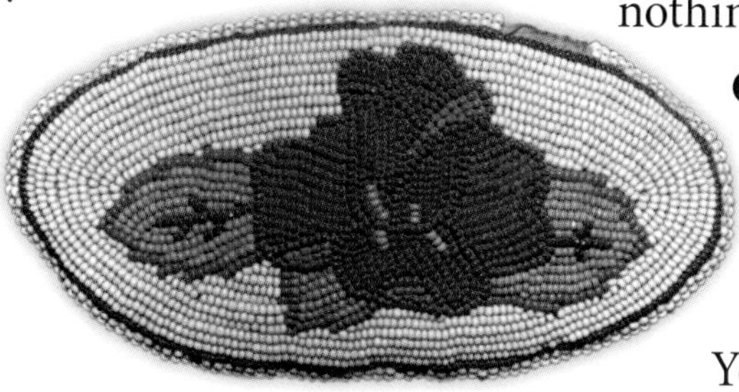

Charbonneau: Shut your mouth! I'm not one of your soldiers.

Ordway: That's for sure. You'd never—

(Clark interrupts.)

Clark: That's enough, you two! Look around. Captain Lewis should be around here. It's been almost a week since he went on ahead.

Charbonneau: Yes, captain.

Peace Offering. *Meriwether Lewis met two Shoshone Indians on August 13, 1805. He gave them beads and other gifts as a sign of peace.*

Ordway: Sorry, captain.

(Clark takes out a spyglass and peers over the landscape.)

Clark: I see people, but I can't tell who they are. Let's move.

(Everyone paddles quickly.)

Ordway: I see them now. There's Shields and McNeal.

Sacagawea: And that's Captain Lewis.

Clark: He's found some Indians. I hope they'll trade with us.

(Sacagawea opens her eyes wide and smiles.)

Clark: What is it?

Sacagawea: Those are— Those are—

Charbonneau: What, what?! Out with it!

Sacagawea: Those—are—my—people.

(Everyone stops paddling and comes ashore.)

Scene 4: Remember Me?

(Clark and his group stand still. Lewis and his men walk toward them. So do Cameahwait (KAH moh wait), Jumping Fish, and any Shoshone extras.)

Lewis: Captain Clark!

Clark: Captain Lewis!

Lewis: All well?

Clark: Yes. And you?

Lewis: Yes indeed.

(Jumping Fish recognizes Sacagawea. She leaps excitedly and then runs to her.)

Jumping Fish: Sacagawea! Is it really you?

Sacagawea: Yes, yes!

Jumping Fish: I didn't think I'd ever see you again.

(The two embrace.)

McNeal: What are they doing?

Cameahwait: Several years ago, the girls were kidnapped. One leaped into a river to escape, so we call her Jumping Fish.

(Both groups come together and hug. The explorers give beads and mirrors to the Shoshone.)

Lewis: I hope we will be friends for years to come.

Clark: Trading will benefit both of us.

Cameahwait: We wish to trade. You need horses, and you may have things we need.

(Sacagawea stares at Cameahwait. Then she races toward him.)

Drouillard: Now what?

Jumping Fish: Our chief is Sacagawea's brother. You have brought them together.

Sacagawea: My family. I waited for this time, but I never thought it would come.

Cameahwait: Sorrow has become joy. Welcome home, sister. Welcome and thanks, new friends.

(Everyone bows.)

Famous Face. *A dollar coin honoring Sacagawea was made in 2000.*

Amazing People
Amazing Expedition

Read their files to find out why.

William Clark

BORN: August 1, 1770, in Caroline County, Virginia

KNOWLEDGE AND SKILLS:
mapmaking, river navigation, trading with Indians

CAREER HIGHLIGHTS:
joined frontier militia (1789); led journey to Pacific Northwest with Meriwether Lewis (1804–06); superintendent of Indian Affairs (1808–38); published trip journals (1814); governor of the Missouri Territory (1813–21)

DIED: September 1, 1838, in St. Louis, Missouri

Meriwether Lewis

BORN: August 18, 1774, near Charlottesville, Virginia

KNOWLEDGE AND SKILLS:
natural history, medicine, geography, and writing

CAREER HIGHLIGHTS:
joined U.S. Army (1794); secretary to President Thomas Jefferson (1801); led journey to Pacific Northwest with William Clark (1804–06); governor of the Louisiana Territory (1807)

DIED: October 10, 1809, near Nashville, Tennessee

Sacagawea

BORN: c. 1788, near the border between Idaho and Montana

KNOWLEDGE AND SKILLS:
Shoshone interpreter, knowledge of how to find food, knowledge of landmarks, symbol of peace

CAREER HIGHLIGHTS:
captured by raiding party and taken away (about 1800); married Toussaint Charbonneau (about 1804); gave birth to a son (February 11, 1805); joined trip to Pacific Northwest (April 7, 1805); saved papers and tools when boat nearly sank (May 14, 1805); reunited with brother Cameahwait (mid-August 1805); saw the Pacific Ocean (November 1805)

DIED: December 20, 1812(?), at Fort Manuel, South Dakota

Crossing New FRONTIERS

Follow Sacagawea's example. Blaze new trails to answer these questions.

1. What were the goals of Lewis and Clark's trip?
2. Who was Sacagawea?
3. At the beginning of the play, why does Lewis want to find Native Americans?
4. Why did the Shoshone chief help Lewis and Clark's team?
5. What did Sacagawea do as part of the team? What did Lewis and Clark do?